THE FOOD GROUPS

NUTRITION BOOKS FOR KIDS

Children's Diet & Nutrition Books

BABY PROFESSOR
EDUCATION KIDS

Speedy Publishing LLC
40 E. Main St. #1156
Newark, DE 19711
www.speedypublishing.com

n this book, we're going to talk about the major food groups. So, let's get right to it!

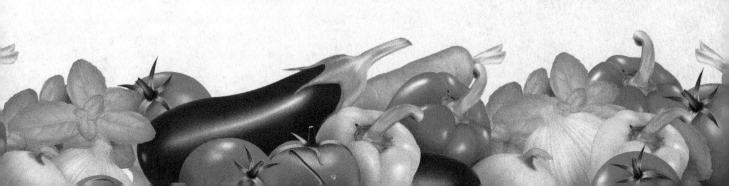

WHAT IS A BALANCED DIET?

Selection of food that is good for the heart.

All human beings need good nutrition in order to stay healthy and live well. When you were a baby, you needed a different diet than you have today. As you get older, the calories you should eat daily and the types of food you should eat change. Younger people who are active and get exercise generally burn off more calories than older people do.

A balanced diet is important. If you ate just carrots for the next six weeks, do you think that would be healthy? What if you ate just chicken for the next month? Both of these foods are healthy for you to eat, but eating them without a balance of other foods over a long period of time isn't a good idea. That's because each type of food has different nutrients. A balanced diet just means that you need a portion of all the different food groups every day to stay healthy and get the proper vitamins and minerals.

Colorful Carrots.

Baked salmon garnished with asparagus and tomatoes with herbs.

Years ago, nutritionists believed that you should eat about the same amount of food from each of the food groups to keep your diet balanced. However, there's a lot more knowledge about nutrition today. It's now recommended that you eat a higher percentage of vegetables, fruits, and grains than of meats and dairy products. All the different groups of foods are important, it's just that you don't need as much food from every group as was previously thought.

WHY IS NUTRITION ESPECIALLY IMPORTANT FOR KIDS?

Most girls stop growing by age 15 and most boys by age 18. However, everyone is different and some adults have continued to grow until their twenties. While you are growing, nutrition is especially important because you need it to ensure your bones and muscles are healthy.

Good nutrition will help you to get to your maximum height and make you strong. If you develop good eating and exercise habits when you're young, you'll give yourself the best opportunity for a long, healthy life.

WHAT ARE THE FOOD GROUPS?

GRAIN

PROTEIN

VEGETABLE

DAIRY

FRUITS

MILK

There are five groups of food that you should eat in your diet daily. They are whole grains, colorful vegetables, fresh fruit, calcium-rich dairy, and lean protein.

Hot 7 Grain Breakfast Cereal With Yogurt
and Fresh Fruit.

GRAINS

All types of breads, most types of pasta, oatmeal, breakfast cereals, hominy grits, and flour tortillas are all examples of different types of grains. Grains are any type of food that is made with rice, cornmeal, oats, barley, wheat, or other types of cereal grains.

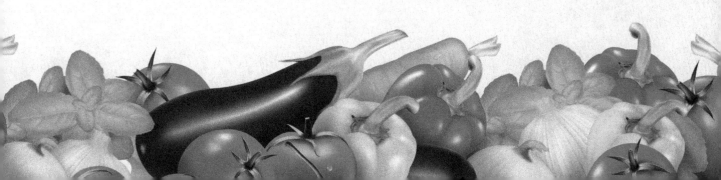

There are two categories within the group of grains—whole grain products and refined grain products. When you buy bread at the store, it will be marked to tell you whether it's whole grain or not.

Whole grain products are made of the entire kernel of grain, which includes the bran, the germ, and the endosperm. For example, brown rice and whole-grain pasta are two examples of whole grain products.

Oat flakes, seeds and bran.

Carbohydrates

Refined grains have been milled differently and during the milling process the bran and germ are removed. This gives refined grain bread and other products a finer texture. In general, refined grain products last longer without spoiling than whole-grain, but they also have less fiber and less of other important nutrients like iron and B-vitamins. White bread and white rice are examples of refined grains.

Some refined grain products are enriched, which means that B-vitamins, such as folic acid, niacin, riboflavin, and thiamin, have been added in after processing. Sometimes iron is added in too. If these have been added, it should be marked *"enriched"* somewhere on the package.

According to the nutritional requirements from the United States Department of Agriculture, USDA for short, everyone should eat at least 50% of their grains as whole grains.

Foods high in carbohydrates

Healthy Foods

VEGETABLES

There are so many different kinds of vegetables that they can be organized into five different categories.

- DARK-GREEN VEGETABLES, like Spinach and Broccoli

- STARCHY VEGETABLES, like Corn and White Potatoes

- RED AND ORANGE VEGETABLES, like Carrots and Sweet Potatoes

- BEANS AND PEAS, like Black Beans and Kidney Beans

- OTHER VEGETABLES, like Cauliflower and Celery

FRUITS

There are many different types of fruits and berries. Apples, peaches, pears, bananas, strawberries, and blueberries are examples of fruits. Tomatoes and avocadoes are technically fruits too since they have seeds, although we generally consider them vegetables. Any type of fruit as well as juices that are 100% fruit juice are good healthy foods from the fruit group. You can prepare and eat fresh fruit, canned or frozen fruit, or dried fruit like raisins or prunes.

MILK AND OTHER DAIRY

This group includes all milk products and many foods made from milk, such as yogurt and cheese. These products all contain calcium, which is important for building bones. Soymilk that has been fortified with calcium is included too, but cream cheese and butter made from milk have almost no calcium so they're not included.

Dairy Products

It's good to choose fat-free or low-fat choices in this group, otherwise the fat they contain adds too much fat to your diet.

Assortment of healthy protein source and body building food.

PROTEIN

All types of meats fit in this category. There are other types of foods that fit here too. Here are some examples of proteins:

- Beef, like steaks and ground beef

- Pork, like pork tenderloin and pork chops

- Poultry, like chicken and turkey

- Seafood, like salmon and tuna

- Nuts, like almonds and walnuts

- Eggs, like chicken eggs and quail eggs

BEANS, PEAS, AND LENTILS

Beans and peas are a special case of unique foods. They contain protein and they also contain a lot of fiber. Vegetarians don't eat meats, so they get most of their protein from beans, peas, and lentils instead. Examples of foods in this group are pinto beans, black-eyed peas, and garbanzo beans.

Assortment of Beans

HOW MUCH OF EACH FOOD GROUP SHOULD YOU EAT?

The USDA has a picture that shows about how much of each food group you should eat every day. In general, the food you eat daily should be about these percentages of your total food intake:

- GRAINS, 30%

The New Food Pyramid.

- VEGETABLES, 40%

- FRUITS, 10%

- PROTEIN, 20%

You should also have a full glass of milk or a cup of yogurt every day.

Nutrition Facts

Serving Size 1 Medium (118 g)

Amount Per Serving

Calories 105   Calories frome Fat 4

% Daily Value *

Total Fat 0.39g	1%
Saturated Fat 0.132g	1%
Trans Fat	
Cholesterol 0mg	0%
Sodium 1mg	0%
Total Carbohydrate 26.95mg	9%
Dietary Fiber 3.1g	12%
Sugar 14.43g	
Protein 1.29g	

Vitamin A   2% • Vitamin C   17%

Calcium   1% • Iron   2%

*Percent Daily Values are based on a 2,000 calorie diet.
Your daily values may be higher or lower depending on
your calorie needs.

SERVING SIZES FOR THE DIFFERENT FOOD GROUPS

Depending on your age and physical activity, the amount of food you eat will vary a little. When people get overweight, the reason frequently is because they serve themselves two or three times the serving size they should be eating. Here are some general guidelines for serving sizes in each food group.

GRAINS

You should be eating a 6-ounce serving of grains every day and half of that amount should be whole grains. A bread slice is about one ounce. A measuring cup of breakfast cereal or half a measuring cup of rice, pasta, or cereal that's been cooked is about one ounce too.

Fresh Bread and Wheat

High Fiber Food for Healthy Eating.

VEGETABLES

The more colorful your vegetables are, the more nutrients they have. You should eat about 2 ½ measuring cups of vegetables that are dark green or orange everyday. Part of your serving can include beans, peas, or lentils too.

FRUITS

You should eat lots of different kinds of fruit, about 2 measuring cups every day. Be careful not to drink too much fruit juice. It's better to eat fresh fruit because it has fiber.

Fruits and Vegetables

DAIRY

Choose dairy products, such as milk or yogurt, that are either fat-free or low-fat. Lots of people are lactose-intolerant, which simply means their digestive systems bother them if they consume milk. You can substitute lactose-free products, like soymilk, that have been fortified with calcium. For kids between the ages of 2 and 8, the proper serving size is about 2 measuring cups of milk or yogurt. Adults can have an additional cup.

Dairy Products

PROTEIN

You should select lean meats and poultry, which means the meats you pick shouldn't have much fat. For example, a piece of grilled chicken with no skin is better than an all-beef hot dog or a burger. You should eat about 5 ½ ounces of protein every day. Some of your serving of protein can include beans, peas, or lentils.

Proteins

GUIDELINES FOR FATS, SALT, AND SUGARS

It's difficult to eliminate all fats, salt, and sugars from your diet. Most of the fat sources you eat should come from natural fats, like vegetable or olive oil, fish, and nuts. Solid fats, like margarine, butter, and shortening, are not healthy or nutritious so it's good to limit the amount you eat.

Healthy Fats: salmon, avocado, oil, nuts

Sugary drinks can make you gain weight and they don't have any nutritional value. Sodas that are sugar-free have other artificial ingredients that aren't healthy either. Water, iced tea, and fruit juice in small amounts are good beverage choices.

Colorful Smoothies

Smartphone Calorie Counter Application

WHAT ARE CALORIES?

Calories are a measurement of the amount of energy that is in our food. Most kids who are still growing need about 2,000 calories a day to stay healthy. If you are too heavy for your age, you might need to limit the number of calories you eat every day to get back to a healthy weight. Eating the recommended serving sizes will help you eat the right amount of foods every day.

Awesome! Now you know more about the food groups and what you should eat to be healthy. You can find more Diet and Nutrition books from Baby Professor by searching the website of your favorite book retailer.

Vegetable Salad

CPSIA information can be obtained
at www.ICGtesting.com
Printed in the USA
LVHW051336040622
720440LV00006B/505